POETRY AND CAPPUCCINO

Frank Barone

eFrog Press

To the friends who have shared their time for coffee,
their smiles, laughter, and love of poetry.

FOREWORD

How does a journey begin? With me it started with a writing workshop. Frank Barone, a mentor teacher, encouraged us to write with our students by modeling this process. We shared and got to know each other. With my young students I used a poem I had written for the first day of school, as Frank had suggested. It helped set the tone for a happy and productive year. To capture our ideas we carried our journals everywhere we went.

Retirement came for me earlier than expected. To fill some of my leisure hours I frequented a coffee shop. One day strolling into the shop I thought I recognized Frank. I boldly asked if he used to teach writing. He said yes and we started talking and haven't stopped.

Frank shared his poems and stories and encouraged me to continue writing. "Keep it simple, cut out extra words, use your senses, make word-pictures, edit, rewrite, and continue to read." Sentence by sentence my writing improved. In sharing our words we have traveled together spending time laughing, drinking coffee, and living our lives.

Now we invite you to step into our world, slow down, notice the rich scents, hear the voices, see what's around you, and enjoy the journey.

—Barbara Abbott

PREFACE

Poets play with words.

Since my retirement as a high school English teacher more than twenty years ago, I continue to play with words in my favorite playground, the local coffee shop. In this environment I see poems by looking out through the window, watch poems walk into the room, touch, taste, and smell poems in the cups of cappuccino I order, and hear poems in the background music, in conversations with friends, or the talk at nearby tables. These same friends listen to and read my poems and encourage me to continue this challenging, productive, and playful activity.

Now I encourage you to join my friends and read these poems for some pleasurable moments at your local coffee shop or favorite playground.

CONTENTS

THEY COME HERE

They come here not just for coffee
but for many different reasons.
Some come to work on their lap-top computers
some for business sessions or job interviews
others for tutoring lessons or to study for exams.
But for the most part they come here
to take a break from home or work
to socialize with friends
meet new people
or to work on a novel
read a book
or page through the newspaper.
Some come just to enjoy the relaxed quiet time
sip a latte, think, and listen to the music.
I come for a cappuccino
and to observe all these people
to see if I can find a poem somewhere on their faces
or in their conversations
or even at times in the distinctive clothes they wear
or the tattoos they display.
It doesn't take much to get me started.
I enjoy the challenge of building a poem
from just a few words, a look, a gesture,
or the trace of an emotion.
Next time you wander into this place
look for me.
I'll be the one sitting in the far corner with my cappuccino
the warmth of the sun on my back
a writing pad on the table
and a Number 2 pencil in my hand.

PERMANENT RESIDENT

The red Ford sedan parked outside
had a New York—The Empire State—license plate.
And here we sit, that car and I,
at a coffee shop in San Diego
the visitor just passing through
soaking up some southern California sunshine
and I, a permanent resident now for over forty years.
Seeing that license plate reminded me of my home town
with its historic Hudson River
lazy Long Island beaches
crowded Times Square and Manhattan theaters
Brooklyn's Bridge and once beloved baseball team
stickball in the streets
subways, trolleys, and sandlots
where we grew up from childhood playmates
into teammates and adults.
Don't get me wrong.
I love sunny San Diego with its easy-paced life style
where I found both my wife and my life
raised a family
made friends
grew in my profession
and now enjoy a comfortable retirement.
I have good memories of New York
better ones, though, from right here.
After a while I watch the New York car
pull out of its parking space
and head for wherever it wants to go.
But I'll continue to sit here
content with my cappuccino
the comforting sunshine
and my California license plates.

HOW FORTUNATE I AM

The past continues to pop up
most of the time in the morning
but also at other quiet times during the day.
Not the whole past, of course,
just small persistent glimpses
of mistakes and misdeeds
regrets and guilt
harsh words spoken and those left unsaid.
But soon my friends Sunshine and Music enter the scene
with their smiles and laughter.
Before long, and for the rest of the day,
those friends accompany me to shopping centers and book stores
to golf courses and on leisurely walks through the neighborhood.
Then Poetry and Reading join us at my favorite coffee house
for an afternoon cappuccino and many pleasurable moments
while they invite me to imagine and create
and to look into the lives of characters
whose stories always offer hope and redemption.
In the evening, at home, and just before I fall asleep,
I give thanks for these and other companions
who remind me how fortunate I am
to have each day's pleasant memories to dream upon.

ALL IN FAVOR

I am all in favor
of frequent and open acts of affection
whether between teenagers hungry for acceptance
who wrap their arms around each other
or between middle-aged couples
secure in their relationships
like the ones I saw today
who embraced
whispered words that brought smiles and laughter
and then spontaneous kisses
while they waited for the coffees they had ordered.
I am convinced
we need more public displays of affection.
We have altogether too many
bold and defiant acts of violence.

THIS PLACE

She would have loved this place
the cheerful servers who would greet her with a smile
and call her by her first name
the way they always welcome me,
the relaxed atmosphere
and the friends she would make here
just the way I have.
She would have looked forward
to cappuccino and conversation
about books and movies and poetry and music
religion, education, sports, the weather
and added her laughter to make each visit
a pleasant experience.
Most of all she would have loved
to have met her grown daughter and son at this place
to have heard about their day
and especially to have hugged her young grandson
whom she had never seen.
But while she would have loved
cappuccino and conversation
all of us realize how happy she must be
and how she must smile
every time she sees her family enjoying our time together
here at this place.

LEISURE TIME

Her knitted purple hat
rests regally on her gray head
like a crown fit for a queen
or a teacher, retired now,
who has earned the right to sit at a table
drink from her coffee
and read all the pages of the New York Times
at her leisure
without any concern about bells or grades
schedules or meetings
or fifth grade adolescent behavior
or parental problems, real or imaginary.
And so I tip my own blue baseball hat to her
I who also retired from teaching
and who comes here to sip my cappuccino
read the stories in the faces of people
and write these poems that enrich my leisure time.

TAKE A BREAK

In her gray business suit
of tight skirt, tailored jacket
and impressively high heels
she enters stage left
trailing her heavy black briefcase
orders her coffee
sits at a table
opens her laptop
and begins to type
or rather, continues her work
of multitasking from computer
to notebook, to answering her cell phone
to off-set any guilty pleasure
of an afternoon coffee break.

AN ERA LONG AGO

We hardly see fedoras anymore
yet here comes this tall gray-haired gentleman
wearing his soft brown hat
pulled toward the back of his head
as if to say, "Take a look at me.
Look past my wire-rimmed glasses
into my clear gray eyes
so you can read the story of my life."
He sits at ease in the deep leather chair
coffee in hand
inviting any of us to draw a mental picture
or a poetic image of him.
I accept this silent invitation
because I'd like others to see him
when they read this poem
so they may remember an era long ago
when gentlemen wore fedoras
and removed them in the presence of ladies
in a gesture of respect.
Times change.
We hardly see fedoras anymore
or gestures of respect
yet the need to act like gentlemen remains
and should be shown through any small act
to acknowledge the presence of ladies in our lives.

ANY SIDEWALK CAFÉ

While it hardly measures up
to the ambience one would find
at any sidewalk café
along the Champs Élysées
the Left Bank
or in quaint Montmartre
with its outdoor art displays
I can still enjoy my cappuccino
at my favorite neighborhood coffee shop
and dream of Paris once again.

A CUP OF JOY

Who will bring me a cup of joy
overflowing with laughter?
And who will play some music
to fill the lonely hours of my life
or sing a song to make my eyes sparkle
and my heart smile?
Who will dance with me
to help chase away today's sorrows
and yesterday's memories?
Will anyone walk a less traveled road
in search of adventure and surprise?
Perhaps someone will take time to write a poem
then share a cappuccino.
We could read our poems to each other
and let the images and rhythm of our words
soothe the ache in our hearts
and restore a moment of calm and order
in our troubled lives.
When you finish your poem
come visit with me.
I will be waiting for you
here in the coffee shop.

A FRENZY OF MOVEMENT

Bees swarm around a purple bush
in front of my favorite coffee shop.
In a frenzy of movement
they spin and swirl
dash and dance
above, below, and in between
the flowers and leaves
in search of a place to build their hive
or perhaps looking for a quick cappuccino
or in need of a soothing café au lait.

MUCH MORE

They make my cappuccino
just the way I like it.
And with their smiles
sense of humor
cheerful laughter
efficient and friendly service
no one can blame me
if I hang out here
to relax, read and write
listen to and talk with friends
and otherwise fill part of my afternoons
with comfortable pleasant memories.
They serve much more here than just coffee.

THE NAME I GAVE HIM

Tex, the name I gave him,
moseyed in for a drink
wearing his high-crowned Stetson
low over his cold gray eyes
and scuffed his pointed brown boots
across the tiled floor.
Instead of a holster at his hip
he wore a small hand-worked leather case on his belt
where he packed his cell phone.
He sat down near me with his back against the wall
just like the gunslingers used to do
in all those Western movies and novels.
I waited to see how fast he could whip out that cell phone
and speed dial his next victim.
But no one made a play or called his number
so Tex just finished his drink
eased his lanky body out of his chair
snaked his way past the tables
then pushed through the swinging doors
and faded into the night.

WOMAN WITH SHORT GRAY HAIR

While she waits for her tall latte
near the counter
the woman with short gray hair
tunes herself into the soft mellow sounds
of cool jazz
lifts her arms
snaps her fingers
and bebops along with the music
to the smiles and silent applause
of this one observer
who would celebrate her joy
within this poem.

READING ROBERT BLY

College-age young man
reclines on the soft leather chair
inside the coffee shop
with his feet outstretched
and his left elbow propped upon the arm rest.
In that same left hand he holds up a book of poems
by the poet Robert Bly.
Only his eyebrows show above the top of the book
so I cannot see whether the words from Bly's poems
brighten his eyes with their images
surprise them with metaphors
sear them with the flames of Truth
or turn them cold as steel
with well-placed shafts of irony.
Then again he may only be reading Robert Bly
as an assignment
for a class
and just for a grade
the cruelest irony of all.

SERVICE POODLE SPEAKS

"Are you looking at me?
You looking at me?
You never seen a service poodle before?
So what if I'm the size of a shoe box.
It's not size that counts, you know.
Mess with me and I'll rip out your toe nails.
I know I look cute
but don't let my pink and green polka-dotted outfit
fool you.
This old lady I work for needs attention
and she gets her kicks by dressing me up
in these crazy-colored, back warmers
that make me want to throw up.
But I'm just doing my job, see?
So take a good look.
Have your laughs.
Then move it, buddy,
before I piddle on your pants."

BIG GAME

There must be a high school basketball game on tonight
because the perky blonde cheerleader
with her hair pulled back in a bouncy pony tail
enters the scene with the required smile
dressed in her green-and-white cheerleader jacket
and long green sweat pants.
As part of her required outfit
she sports two male teenage admirers
one on each arm
and dangles them like trophies
in front of the crowd of afternoon coffee drinkers
while she goes over her routines
and practices her moves
for tonight's big game.

THE NOTE BOOK

She sat at a table
sipping from her coffee
and writing in her notebook.
And if her short gray hair
the dark spots on her hands
and the support-hose she wore
underneath her checkered slacks
were not enough to show her age,
the way she wrote each letter of every word
in her lined composition note book
in perfect Palmer Method handwriting
all combined to reveal not just an older woman
but one who belonged to a generation
that valued precision and took pride
in the lessons learned in school.

ONE MAN BAND

Gray-haired gentleman
sits outside the coffee shop
and hugs his ukulele
against his blue Hawaiian shirt
while his eyes scan the sheet of music
on the table in front of him
and his fingers graze the strings
of this instrument he loves
so only he can hear the notes
that carry him across the Pacific
and onto the warm sands of an island Paradise.

THE LATEST FASHION

Young woman with short blond hair
Enters the shop
dressed in the latest fashion:
a matching slacks-and-jacket outfit
of green and gray desert camouflage.
She asks for coffee
and when she receives her order
she steps out the door and into the sunshine.
Soon she will be deployed to the war zone
in the Middle East
where she will encase her short blond hair
in a close-fitting helmet
and join the other young men and women
who blend in with the environment
dressed in their green and gray desert camouflage.

USURPER

The young man with uncombed hair
sits at what I have come to consider
my personal corner table
and sips from his Perrier.
I find it easy, however,
to forgive this usurper
when I notice the title of the book
that holds his attention:
The Collected Poems of C. P. Cavafy.
Anyone who sips Perrier
and reads Cavafy
must possess a high degree of culture
and wins, for this day at least,
not only my admiration
but my personal corner table.

HOLY ORDER

The good nun
glides noiselessly
into this shop
and orders a café au lait
to satisfy her only vice.

FROM MY TABLE

I didn't have to turn around
from my table
to realize the blond, young woman
wearing sunglasses and a red dress
that revealed her tanned shoulders
had taken a seat immediately behind me.
Her industrial strength perfume
gave her away.

HOMELESS

We used to call them "hoboes"
a somewhat romantic term
for those who rode the rails whenever they wanted
to whatever town they wished to go.
We called others "bums"
a rather derogatory classification
for those who begged on street corners
or from door to door
or whom we found asleep or worse
at curb sides or in darkened alleyways.
Now we employ a more pleasant sounding word
for those unfortunate men, women, and even children
caught between poverty and hunger
rejection and loneliness.
The homeless young man I saw yesterday
outside the coffee shop
used his reflection in the plate glass window like a mirror
to groom himself.
He ran dirt-caked fingers through beard and hair
then placed a soiled knitted cap on his head
and all the while he kept up a conversation with himself
to keep from feeling lonely.
Satisfied with his appearance
and still engaged in a one-sided dialogue
he walked away down the street
toward whatever cardboard box or makeshift shelter
he called home.

LIPSTICK

The young server behind the counter
took the time during her morning makeup
to apply a touch of lipstick
to enhance her ready smile
like the swirls of strawberry
on top of the sweet tasting pastry.

CALIFORNIA COWGIRL

Middle-aged California cowgirl
sporting a ten-gallon hat
tee shirt
denim shorts
and open-toed sandals
sashays into the coffee shop
for a low-fat latte.
I suppose she parked her surfboard
at the hitching post.

BALANCING ACT

Bearded biker
peddles his way
along the busy city street
and steers with one hand
while in the other hand
he holds both
his super-sized soft drink
and his opened umbrella
to keep the San Diego sun
from doing damage
to his delicate complexion.

NATURAL BEAUTY

In the patio area
outside the coffee shop
a young woman
with just the hint of makeup
to enhance her large gray eyes
and otherwise natural beauty
enjoys a cappuccino and some conversation
with her companion.
And when a curious toddler
hands pressed against the window
stares at her from inside the shop
the young woman
manages just the beginning of a smile
as she sits confined to her wheelchair.

THIS THEATER

Macbeth had his three witches
but this theater has its three elegant
gray-haired ladies
whose eye glasses help them
to notice each other
in the fading afternoon sunlight
as they sit at a table by the window
and share their friendship
along with their coffee.
They wear no pointed hats
stir no witches' brew
intone no sorceress' chant about toil and trouble.
They only come to treat themselves
to a pleasant hour together
as a diversion from household chores
and busy schedules.
Finished with their meeting and coffee
these three ladies rise gracefully
and exit this theater, stage left,
while I silently applaud their grand performance
with this poem.

DOUBLE TREAT

He sits at a table
and treats himself to some quiet time
an iced tea
and a good book to read.
But more than this
he picks up his cell phone
calls his mother
and treats her to fifteen minutes
of listening and conversation
beginning with "Hi, Mom.
How are you?"
and closing with
"Goodbye, Mom. I love you."

THE CONVERSATION

Mother and child
sat at the small table
and while her daughter sipped from her drink
played with her toy
and made delightful but unintelligible sounds
the mother pulled out her cell phone
and talked and laughed and talked and talked
and ignored her daughter's infant attempts
at conversation.
The mother never heard her daughter's
playful giggle and pleasant sounds
as serious requests for attention and love.
Mother only continued to talk and laugh
and talk some more.
And I wondered if years from now
the mother will ever listen
to her teenage daughter's cries for help
when her phone rings late at night.

MILES FROM WOODSTOCK

Two people stepped into the room
right out of the '60's
two latter-day hippies
with their identifying long hair
love beads and sandals
he with his gray goatee
she with her earth-tone clothes.
They sat side by side at the same table
drank from their coffees
and looked at the drawings in his sketch book.
Though far away from Haight-Ashbury
and even more miles from Woodstock
this neighborhood shop
would make a friendly gathering place
for anyone in search of love and peace
or just a comfortable cup of coffee.

FRED AND GINGER

Unlike Ginger Rogers
this woman wore dark-rimmed glasses.
And unlike Fred Astaire
this man had sandals on his otherwise bare feet.
She didn't glide about in an evening gown
and he didn't dash around in a tuxedo.
But when the middle-aged couple stood
held each other
and began to sway
to Ella Fitzgerald's bouncy ballad
they transformed the cramped space
between the tables and chairs of the coffee shop
into any one of those movie-set night club dance floors
in any one of those memorable musicals
that featured the graceful talents of Fred and Ginger.
When Ella's song ended
one of the customers applauded their performance.
The couple smiled, bowed, and returned to their seats
where they resumed their previous anonymous identities.

RENDEZVOUS

It became obvious to me
the more I listened to their conversation
that the adult couple at the table nearby
had come here to meet for the first time
and share pleasantries about their lives
over coffee
to see if they could be compatible enough
for a second meeting
or even a longer relationship.
But perhaps one cup of coffee
would be enough for either one of them
to pierce through any pretense
and then decide to move along   .
thank you anyway
to another time
another place
another possible rendezvous.

GAME PLAN

At this neutral site
two disgruntled mothers
meet with the glib team coach
over cups of coffee
to listen to him explain away
any perceived injustice done to their sons.
And while I overhear his blather of clichés
and predictable offensive and defensive arguments
it becomes apparent he has used this game plan before
on other concerned and offended parents
and more than likely
and still more unfortunately
he will use it again and again
and so continue to add to his winning record.

TWO YOUNG LADS

Two young lads celebrate
the end of the school year
and the beginning
of summer vacation
by pedaling their bicycles down the hill
and across the busy intersection
to sit at an outside table
and drink and slurp their vanilla milks
in an unspoken toast to friendship and freedom.

BUSINESS MEETING

Business meeting over coffee
involves four listeners
and one dominant
incessant
relentless
strident speaker
who leaves no doubt among her co-workers
how the business should be run
and by whom.

TEAMWORK

Two elderly women
sit opposite each other
at a table
drink their coffee
and work on their crossword puzzles.
When they come upon a difficult DOWN
or an unknown ACROSS
they consult each other
until they finish their coffee
and complete this day's mental exercise.

STUDY GROUP

The local hospital's study group
of aides and interns
meets this sunny December day
to talk about arteries, lungs,
the aorta, and ventricles
while they drink their coffees
listen to the piped-in holiday songs
of Tony Bennett and Nat King Cole
and laugh at silly jokes and funny stories
before they return to their work
of healing the sick
and comforting the dying.

COFFEE BREAK

Middle-aged couple
sit at a sun-lit window table
sip their coffee
and read from their books.
They have all they need
to enjoy this afternoon interlude.
Most of all
they have each other.

TODAY'S LESSON

At a corner table inside the coffee shop,
not the most ideal study situation,
a young woman tutors a teenage student
about Hannibal, Rome, and Carthage
when the boy's mother strides in
stands at the table
barely acknowledges the tutor
and listens to a brief teacher-student exchange.
The lesson over
the lad, backpack weighted on his shoulders,
follows his mother toward the door.
The boy starts to say something
when the mother turns and snaps,
"I don't want to hear any more of your excuses."
With her son slouching behind her
she marches out the door
without even ordering a latte.

FATHERS AND SONS

Never had a real conversation with my father.
Never had any heart-to-heart talks
or "How's it going? What's on your mind?"
kind of discussion.
 He'd get angry. Shout.
I'd withdraw. Silent.
Years have passed
but the memory came back a few days ago
when my son phoned and asked
if I'd like to get a cup of coffee.
We sat outside a local shop.
He talked about his work
his friends
about baseball and golf.
I listened. Made some comments.
We both shared a few laughs
along with the coffee.
I watched a blue heron spread her wings
and fly out of a nearby tree.
I saw her return
and pointed her out to my son.
I hope these will be the memories he recalls
years from now:
how much we enjoyed our coffee
our conversations
and the blue heron who spread her wings in flight
and added more beauty
to our lives together.

IN MY NEXT POEM

So where will my next poem come from?
Perhaps from the sunlit street in front of my favorite coffee shop
where I can look out and watch the passing cars
and the people walking by.
Or from the conversations I overhear as I sit at my table
or even from the silent messages I receive
from those who sit alone
with only their thoughts and caffeinated drinks
to keep them company
or from the drama I observe between couples
who sit across from each other.
The next poem could come from the pages of the book I am reading
when the words and metaphors create pictures that brighten my eyes
and stir my imagination.
Music from the overhead speakers
the cheerful, busy servers
the colorful and sometimes odd clothes worn by customers
yesterday's memories
or tomorrow's possibilities
will sometimes initiate the writing process.
The blank page does not remain empty for too long
whenever my true subject reveals itself or surprises me
and demands that I listen to its story
and insists that I bring it to the attention of others
in my next poem.

WHAT ED ASKED ME

Just met Ed
war veteran, retired math teacher
a good guy with a great smile
pleasant laugh, and friendly personality.
After our introduction Ed asked me,
"Where do the words come from?
How do you find the words for a poem?"
My response: read a lot.
Fill your well with words.
Mechanics work with tools.
Poets work with words and play with language.
It also helps to keep your senses open
alert to see a hummingbird
and see its wings fluttering into your imagination
with possibilities
to feel the strength of a compassionate embrace
the smell of lilacs recalling a young boy's neighborhood
the taste of bitter memories or happy moments.
Now play with those words.
Arrange them along the lines
until they fit tightly together
and move with ease and rhythm
like Fred Astaire and Ginger Rogers across the dance floor
until the music of the poem ends
and the words glide gracefully off the page
into the eyes and hearts of their audience.
Poems sometimes come from meeting people like Ed
who make it easy for poets to find the words
in a smile, a laugh, a friendly personality.

BUILDING MEMORIES

We like to hang out together
him with his vanilla milk
and his eleven-year-old enthusiasm
for basketball
me with my cappuccino
and long-time passion for golf.
We'll talk about his San Diego adventures
and my New York neighborhoods
his school-day highlights
and my encounters with metaphors
and possible poems.
With every meeting we have at home
at the recreation center, on the golf course
or here in the coffee shop
Charlie and I continue to build memories
and deepen our relationship
as loving grandson
and his ever grateful grandfather.

CONTINUING EDUCATION

Three youngish ladies
and one not so young
sit at a table near mine
where they drink their coffee
share laughter and personal stories
just loud enough for the whole room to hear.
Their laughter shows they enjoy each other's company
and their stories reinforce the friendships they have nurtured
since they first met in some classroom
as three young students
and one not so young teacher.
They have come together this time
not only for coffee
but to create a book club
so they will have more opportunities
to laugh, exchange stories,
and continue their enthusiasm for reading
their love of learning
and their friendships
beyond the walls of any classroom.

FOR JOHN, THE WRITER

I sit here
sip from my cappuccino
and hold his stories in my hands
stories with words that flow
dance, lift, soar, and coax me
to read line after line
page after page
filled with simple and profound truths
honest words and metaphors that surprise my eyes
touch my heart and entice my imagination
to continue to explore his gift of finding ideas
in a bed, a well, a town, the night, a mermaid
or anywhere and anyplace his creative eyes may discover
a beginning he can develop with a middle
that pulls me toward a thoughtful end.
These stories have come to me at this Christmas season
a perfect time for sharing gifts
and so I return the favor with this poem
written from a heart respectful of his talent
thankful for his friendship.

GET INTO YOUR GROOVE

No matter how old you may be
don't be afraid to get up
onto any dance floor,
kitchen area, carpeted living room,
street corner, or the tiled surface
of your favorite coffee shop
where you can get into your groove
with some hip-hop, bebop, or doo-wop steps
make some mellow moves to swing music
or slow dance with your favorite partner.
Dancing reminds us to let go of troubles and worries
lighten up our mood and spirit
and allows our bodies to exercise some muscle memory
of younger days when we partied at proms
or jumped up and down on gym floors at sock hops.
Dancing tells us not to let frustration
lead to depression
but to give nimble feet and eager hips
the chance to make us smile a little
and restore some joy to our lives.
So play the music and show us your steps
in the kitchen or living room
on the street corner
or at the make-believe ballroom
of your favorite coffee shop.

HER COMPANIONS

Young lady opened the door
stepped inside
and fell to the floor.
She lay there for a moment without a sound
until her companion asked her,
"Are you okay?"
She answered, "I'm okay,"
and proceeded to roll onto her side
placed her hands on the floor
and began to lift her body and stand upright.
Only then did I notice
the braces she had on her legs
as she moved to the counter to order her drink.
Cup in hand
she walked to seat herself at a table
with her companion.
With every step she took on that journey
I admired her for her other two companions:
her composure and her courage.

IN SEARCH OF ANY CRUMBS

Thin sparrow
hops across the patio
at our local coffee shop
in search of any crumbs she may find
to give her the energy to lift her weakened wings
and fly back to her nest
to feed and tend to her young ones.
Thin sparrow
presents me with a symbol
and offers me the metaphor I need
to write this poem about world hunger.

MY DAUGHTER, TERI

After her frequent strolls through shopping malls
in search of sales or any colorful item
for her husband and growing son
my daughter, Teri, will sometimes
meet with me before heading home.
Our friends at this coffee shop
always return her cheerful greetings
grateful, as I am,
for every visit with her.
Years ago Teri came into our lives with a smile
and she continues to uplift us with her laughter
lighten our troubles with her joy
and charm our hearts
with the gift of her presence.

OCEAN, SKY, EARTH

Vast, deep ocean
waits at the edge of shore
teases us with playful waves
invites us to splash in its surf
and challenges us to search beneath its waters
for as yet undiscovered poems
hidden inside encrusted shells
poems held fast in the hulls of sunken ships
or those poems with the freedom to swim and explore
in any direction they choose.

Silent, blue sky
pleads with us to notice
the many gifts it offers us each day
the warm friendship of sunshine
the presence of stars and moon at night
clouds to intrigue our imaginations
and rain to encourage growth
and satisfy our thirst for poems.

Firm, fertile earth
surrounds us with the strength of mountains
serene lakes and busy streams
comforts us with trees whose leaves whisper secrets to each other
and sing silent songs only poets and dreamers may hear
a land peopled with old poems
poems newly written and those not yet born
who wait for any poet to discover them
write them into existence
and give them a voice and strength
to travel across oceans
reach the stars and moon
and touch the hearts of all of us
who journey upon this earth.

PURPLE BLOUSE

I held the door open
at the coffee shop
for the white-haired woman
confined to her wheelchair.
Her companion
who wheeled her through
thanked me for my assistance.
The elderly woman
also thanked me
but without any words
only by the gratitude
in her eyes and her smile
and in the way her purple blouse
brightened both her life
and mine.

SECOND HOME

Large, bearded man
wears a dull red parka
over his hooded gray sweatshirt.
When he comes to visit, he prefers to sit at an outside table.
After he eats his small snack
he then reenters the coffee shop
to refresh himself in the restroom
before he leaves to return
down the street toward the barely visible path
that leads into the trees and dense brush
and the company of his other homeless companions.

SONG AND DANCE

Get up on your feet
up on your toes
down on your heels
step and slide
shake and glide
sway from side to side
bend those knees
twist those hips
swing your arms
and let the rhythm flow
into your soul
and carry you out of this world
into a heaven on earth
bright with smiles
warm with love and laughter.
Now sing those words
that fit the music
and fill the room
with resonant poetry
and see and hear and feel
the way those tones
lift your spirits
blend with your movements
and show us
the freedom and joy and pleasure
that comes through this gift
of song and dance.

STILL POPULAR

Sing your songs, Louis Prima.
Keep putting some bounce
some rhythm and harmony
into my life.
Let the music of your band
invite my feet to dance
and my heart to smile.
I like the way you have fun with the lyrics
the way you improvise and play with words
and the way your band backs up your singing
with its lively jazz style
still popular after all these years.
Thank you, Louis Prima,
for being more than "Just a Gigolo"
for casting me under the spell
of "That Old Black Magic"
and for inviting my feet to dance
and my heart to sing.

THE COMFORT OF HIS HAND

With his young son in hand
the father entered the coffee shop
and walked to the counter
until the child pulled away
shrieked his displeasure
at having to share his dad
with customers
and ran toward the door.
Aware of the boy's special needs
the father turned and moved to the exit
offered his young son the comfort of his hand
and stepped outside
without any taste of his desired coffee.

"YOU NEVER GET USED TO IT."

—Anonymous

Of course she spoke the truth
this woman
who overheard my friend ask me
how I had dealt with the death of my wife
almost twenty years ago.
This woman didn't wait for a response
but walked past our table and out the door
of this coffee shop.
She spoke the truth.
We never get used to the absence
of a loved one's presence
the touch of a hand
the warmth of an embrace
the sound of laughter.
These memories sustain us.
My friend and I sat there in silent agreement
with the wisdom of this woman's words between us.
She had probably suffered her own loss
but neither her loss nor mine
meant we could not extend and deepen our love.
Death may take away a loved one's presence
but love can continue to grow
even beyond the grave.

APRIL IN PARIS

Light rain in St. Catherine Square.
I sit in the corner of the Bistro de la Place
look into the mirrored wall
and see the reflection of a Mona Lisa
and paintings of street scenes
along with black and white photographs
of Lauren Bacall, Audrey Hepburn, and Ava Gardner
and I say to my brother, even in black and white
the camera cannot diminish the beauty
of these actresses.
Atop the shelf at the bar, facing the diners,
stand bottles of liquors and cognacs
with rhythmic names like Courvoisier and Napoleon,
bottles filled with history and warmth.
The owner himself comes to take our order
serves me soup
then returns later to chide me
for not finishing the portion he gave me.
Next comes the specialty of the day,
veal cooked in red sauce
and home fried potatoes seasoned with garlic.
With my hunger and taste buds satisfied
I compliment the waiter for this meal
and my two desserts of Irish coffee and Cointreau.
Delighted with my dinner
and with the pleasant atmosphere of the restaurant
I count this other blessing,
the company of my brother
who invited me to come along with him
to experience the sights, the sounds,
and the tastes of Paris in April.

MY CAPPUCCINO FRIENDS

Come with me
and I'll hold the door open for you
at my favorite coffee shop.
As we approach the counter
you'll notice the smiles of the busy servers,
happy to see us and take our orders.
glad to take our orders and serve us.
Before we sit at the table by the window
let me introduce you to some other friends of mine
who come here regularly to relax over coffee
enjoy each others' company and conversation
laugh a little
and perhaps do some reading, writing,
or computer browsing.
Let's take our seats now
so we can sip and savor our coffee.
And notice how the rhythmic background music
adds to the pleasant and casual atmosphere.
When we've finished and get ready to leave
you can hold the door open for me
while I wave and say goodbye
to all my cappuccino friends.

ABOUT THE AUTHOR

A former English teacher, Frank Barone has had his poetry published in local, state, and national journals. As a member of The San Diego Area Writing Project he has consulted and presented on writing for teachers and students at all grade levels.

Since his retirement over twenty years ago, he has continued to write and share his poetry at his favorite coffee shop. He hopes this collection of poems will widen his circle of friends.

76594722R00042

Made in the USA
San Bernardino, CA
13 May 2018